QUOTES
AND ANECDOTES
on how to avoid the
"YEAH BUT SYNDROME"

Tanya L. Martin, Psy.D., L.L.P.

QUOTES
AND ANECDOTES
on how to avoid the
"YEAH BUT SYNDROME"

Copyright © 2009 by Tanya L. Martin, Psy.D., L.L.P.

ISBN 9780615333410

Contents

Dedication

This book is dedicated **to my sister, Leslie**—

For the *person **you were**–*

　　　　the person you ***are**–*

　　　　　　*and the person **you** are **becoming.***

　　　　　　　　　　~I Love You.

Opening Quote

"Let us Summon a New Spirit."

~ Barack Obama,
President of the United States of America

Foreword

"...I am come that you might have life, and that you might have it more abundantly." John 10:10

The above promise from the word of God is a positive affirmation, which says to us that regardless of circumstance or situation, with Christ, life can and shall be abundant. More often than not, we believe the promise to be true, but occasionally there is the emergence of a hesitance that surfaces and chains us to a weight of doubt and disbelief, shackling our joy and derailing us from our destiny.

It is in these times that Dr. Tanya Martin has extended herself to not only be blessed with life, but to be a blessing to all she encounters. Dr. Martin is one who truly exemplifies love and compassion for people; both personally and professionally. She has consciously and conscientiously signed up to be a *"Warrior* and *Aide"* to those who fight for recognition and confirmation of their own self worth. Dr. Martin's work has helped to provide those of us in need with tools to move beyond personal obstacles, barriers, and setbacks.

Through this current literary work, Dr. Martin has given a gentle, yet firm *"push"*, taking us from being stuck within our own rationalizations of our current stagnation, to moving forward with the energy and insight to continue pressing toward the mark of one's own individual calling and purpose.

Jesus walked among us to encourage and to save; Dr. Martin lives her life by much the same credo, as she writes to encourage us and to lead us, to a life altering *positive change*, with the help of– *"Quotes and Anecdotes on How to Avoid the Yeah But Syndrome."*

~Rev. Dr. Laura Foster, Assistant Pastor,
Greater Quinn African Methodist
Episcopal Church, Detroit, Michigan

Preface

Like most children, I remember being asked, "What do you want to be when you grow up?" and like most little girls, I gave a traditional response, often saying, "A teacher or a nurse." I remember providing the same answer until I reached eleven years of age. It was at this point that my life took a turn, and I came upon my desired life's work. You see it was at the ripe age of eleven that I was betrayed and lied upon, by a person I believed to be my best friend. Of course, as a child, I took the lie and accusations painfully, and considered it to be a personal affront and attack. This experience was so devastating that shortly after being told about the lie, I quickly ran home, in hopes of receiving some much needed TLC from my mother. I distinctly remember running into the house and shouting, "Mom! Mom!" as I heard her shout back, *(in a much softer tone)* " What is it? I'm upstairs." I continued my run through the house, as I took two steps at a time, making my way to her upstairs bedroom. When I made it to the top of the stairs, we literally ran into one another, as I was out of breath and she was anxiously asking, "What's the matter!?" It took a second for me to catch my breath, as I simultaneously began to cry and tell her "Carey told a lie on me!" She then told me, "Stop crying, so I can understand what you're saying". I slowly stopped crying, while wiping my tears away, as I began to tell her what happened. My mom listened intently, as I shared the entire story. By the end of the story, with my tears dried and emotions stabilized, I looked at my mother and said, "When I grow up, I want to help people like Carey, who lies on other people...so what kind of job could I get?" I clearly remember my mom looking at me with a great sense of awe, shock and bewilderment, as she appeared to be suppressing a laugh when she said, "It sounds like you might want to be a Psychiatrist." She went on to explain to me exactly what a Psychiatrist does. I accepted her definition and decided that I'd be a Psychiatrist when I grew up.

Introduction

As stated in the **Preface,** I was devoted to becoming a Psychiatrist, until at age thirteen, I listened intently as one of my junior high school teachers provided a lecture on various careers. Surprisingly, when he began to provide the job description of a Psychologist, my two-year steadfast determination to become a Psychiatrist left me, almost as quickly as it came. (A Psychiatrist is a medical doctor and has to attend medical school, and I had no desire or interest in becoming a medical doctor, or attending medical school.) However, a Psychologist felt more fitting for me, because it affords me the opportunity to have a deeper connection and involvement with people and assist them with problem solving. Once I made and understood the distinction between the two, I have not deviated from that career path, as I've earned one undergraduate and three graduate degrees in Clinical Psychology. Consequently, with my educational training and professional expertise, I work as a Clinical Psychologist, College Professor and Certified Imago Relationship Therapist.

My career path has always consisted of direct contact, guidance, assistance and helping others. As a result, I love my work, as I not only help others, but I am also "gifted" with the opportunity to help myself. Therefore, I consider my work a true act of *Divine Reciprocity*.

My work also involves assisting others with making personal *positive change*. However, I am often amazed, when some of my clients and students choose to remain wedded to their negative circumstances, rather than make the *positive change* necessary to improve their lives. After patiently listening to their stories, I usually reflect their stories back to them, to assure that we are on the "same page." Once that is determined, I give my recommendations and advice, in hopes of getting them on the road to *positive change*. Surprisingly, when recommendations for *positive changes* are given, I am frequently interrupted and told, *"Yeah But"*, before being told how they have already tried what I have suggested, and how what I've suggested will not work. Now mind you, this is usually said without the person ever *actively* implementing the recommendations; sadly, this exchange has persisted throughout my career.

Ironically, approximately two years ago, while in session with one of my clients, who had repeatedly and consistently recited, *"Yeah But"*, I distinctly remember saying to him, "I'm going to write a book and I'm going to call it the *"Yeah But Syndrome"*, since you are so quick to tell me, how and why *positive change* will not help or fully improve your situation." My client chuckled as we continued his session. At the conclusion of that session, the idea of writing the book...this book, stayed with me, and each time I met with or talked with someone, and they used those infamous two words, *"Yeah, But"*, I was always taken aback and reminded of the book. Those two words began to crop up so frequently that I began to look at it as a syndrome, which is simply, a consistent pattern of behavior(s).

Consequently, thoughts of writing the book began to slowly consume me, as I found myself quietly and frequently thinking about it. Ironically, during those many thoughtful moments, I found myself succumbing to the very thing that I accused my clients and students of...*"Yeah, But"*, as I, too was making up a myriad of excuses as to why I could not and should not write this book. My most frequently used excuses were, *"I'm not a writer, No one will read it, I don't have the time, I don't have the money, What if I write it and nobody buys it?"* After being repeatedly reminded of my own excuses, I began to realize that it was necessary for me to write this book, in an effort to rid myself of the very thing that I so aptly accused my clients and students of. Therefore, in an effort to practice what I preach, I decided to write this wonderful little book.

In writing this book and sharing one of my own personal experiences of the *"Yeah, But Syndrome"*, it is my heartfelt desire to encourage and share with others, thought-provoking, spirit-moving and *positive change* inducing quotes, anecdotes, phrases and scriptures, on how to effectively avoid, confront and deal with this ALL-consuming syndrome. As a result, this book is comprised of seven chapters, designed to assist—YOU—the reader, on how to do just that. The concept is quite simple—YOU—the reader, are advised to approach the contents of this book with an open heart, mind and spirit, in order to fully receive, embrace and apply the messages. The regular application and incorporation of at least one of the messages on a daily basis, can very well lead to and bring about personal *positive change*, while slowly healing and curing the syndrome. In other words, take your power and energy away from negative thoughts and behaviors, and place them into positive thoughts and behaviors, and watch your life make the *positive change* that you've always dreamed and talked about.

"Make That Change"
~Michael Jackson

I.
Spiritual "Well-Being"

Whether or not you are a **GOD-fearing** child of God, this section of the book can be used as a guide to develop and/or expand upon your own spirituality. So allow yourself to be guided and directed, as I've utilized various quotes from individuals, whom I believe to be "spiritual giants" in their own right. Some of those quoted are used several times, only because their messages repeatedly resonated with me, and it is my hope that they will do the same for you. So go ahead, turn the page, and take your very first step, in ridding yourself of the *"Yeah But Syndrome"*.

"…the impossible can happen to *us*, not somebody else."

~*Andrew Merritt, Pastor*

"Enjoy today and let tomorrow take care of itself."

~*Joyce Meyer, Pastor*

"Next time the devil tries to back you into a corner, get quiet. Ask God to show you the way of escape. He'll bring you out in victory every time."

~*Kenneth Copeland, Pastor*

"There is no need to confer with people, when you have heard from God."

~*Bishop Keith Butler*

"Don't fear the worst, believe the best."

~*Joel Osteen, Pastor*

"Faith is the seed of healing, if you don't plant it, it won't grow."

~*Gloria Copeland, Pastor*

"It's not Satan who's defeating you--it's your openness to him."

~Creflo Dollar, Pastor

"A breakthrough in our spirit always leads to a breakthrough in our lives."

~Phil Pringle, Pastor

"If you don't let go of the old, God can't bring the new."

~Joel Osteen, Pastor

"If you're gonna go forward, you gotta quit looking backwards."

~Joel Osteen, Pastor

"You've got to learn to NOT talk in favor of your problem."

~Dr. Frank Summerfield

"The dark night of the soul is just a part of the process."

~Rev. Shaheerah Stephens

"God ain't tryin' to get you to do something you can do–He's tryin' to get you to do something He can do."

~*Dr. Bill Winston*

"If I will do what I can do, God will do what I can't do."

~*Joyce Meyer, Pastor*

"I trust you God, even when I don't understand you."

~*Paula White, Pastor*

"It's never too late, to begin again."

~*Joyce Meyer, Pastor*

"You can't go to where you want to be and stay where you're at."

~*Joyce Meyer, Pastor*

"When you don't know what to do, be still and wait on God."

~*T.D. Jakes, Pastor*

"We will never change what we tolerate."

~*Joel Osteen, Pastor*

"We don't need a wishbone, we need a backbone."

~*Joyce Meyer, Pastor*

"God can see your heart, but the Devil hears your words."

~*Joyce Meyer, Pastor*

"We have to stop wasting today, trying to figure out tomorrow."

~*Joyce Meyer, Pastor*

"You gotta get out of your own comfort zone."

~*Joel Osteen, Pastor*

"God has to give it to you in the spirit, before it will manifest in the flesh."

~*Rev. Edgar Vann*

"Stand on the Word, until you get your breakthrough."

~*John Francis, Pastor*

"When you have a dream in your heart, you'll see things other people don't see."

~*Joel Osteen, Pastor*

"You can not prepare for defeat and expect to have victory."

~*Joel Osteen, Pastor*

"Don't argue with stupid people, because they've had way more practice than you have."

~*Rev. Nadeer*

"It is only through change that we make progress."

~*Joyce Meyer, Pastor*

"You ain't gon' live no better than you believe."

~*T.D. Jakes, Pastor*

"You have to come against the thing that is coming
against you."

~T.D. Jakes, Pastor

"God would not have put the dream in you, if he had
not already given you the talent."

~Joel Osteen, Pastor

"Change isn't change, until you've changed."

~Creflo Dollar, Pastor

"Whatever we think about and thank about, we bring
about."

~Dr. Denis Watley

"When you face what you fear, you become fearless."

~Lisa Bevere, Pastor

"When you are doing what you are meant to do, your
life makes a difference."

~Freddie Haynes, Pastor

"You have to believe that your words have power."

~*Bishop Ben Gilbert*

"Different is not deficient."

~*Jeremiah Wright, Pastor*

"Most people fear change and treasure the security of where they are."

~*Zachary Tims, Pastor*

"You face your greatest opposition when you are closest to your biggest miracle."

~*T.D. Jakes, Pastor*

"The real issue is self-development."

~ *Noel Jones, Bishop*

"If you want to help God out—get in sync with what He's trying to get you to see."

~*Creflo Dollar, Pastor*

"If you don't know where you're going, you're not gonna
know when you get there."

~Jesse Duplantis, Pastor

"It's not what happens to you that makes one bit of
difference, it's how you respond."

~Joyce Meyer, Pastor

"Instead of waitin' on your gift, why don't you give
one?"

~Rev. Daniel J. Reid

"... You change the circumstances--you don't let the
circumstances change you."

~Rev. Laura E. Foster

"If you can see the invisible, God will do the
impossible."

~Joel Osteen, Pastor

"You don't have to be perfect, to be used by God."

~*Rick Warren, Pastor*

"You can't fulfill your purpose, if you drop off in the pain of the process."

~*Dr. Asa Andrews*

"You must have a willingness to exercise the power of patience."

~*Bishop Ben Gilbert*

"Trust the still sweet sound of
YOUR spiritual voice."
~T.M.

II.
"Everyday" People

Because I've always delighted in learning, both directly and indirectly, from the various people that I encounter on a daily basis, I felt it extremely important to acknowledge them, by documenting their philosophical views in my book. These individuals come from diverse backgrounds; some highly educated, some uneducated, some employed, some underemployed and some unemployed. No matter what their backgrounds are, they share with me a sense of humanness that comes from a place deep within, which speaks to me from a place of truth and authenticity. As a result, they touched my intellect and spirit, in ways that left me thinking... "YES! they get it!", and the "it" that they get is--the importance of making *positive change*. Therefore, I felt it necessary and extremely important, to share their many heartfelt, motivational, inspiring and sincere quotes of wisdom. So please, continue to turn the pages, and check out the wisdom of *"Everyday" People.*

"No one can disrupt what the Lord has planned for you."

~Pamela Crosson, Educator

"We're His tool and if the tool is in the shed, we're not working."

~Helen Jackson, Psychologist

"Until we learn what we need to learn, we keep repeating the same behavior, over and over again."

~Melva Thomas-Johnson, Therapist

"Just ask God to go beyond what your eyes can see."

~Dane', from the Cable TV Program, The Messengers

"My tears don't compromise my strength."

~Anonymous

"I want to change the world and change my life too."

~Lesego, student from Oprah's Leadership Academy

"I use thoughts of strength and love and everything I
think and say comes back to me."

~*Gail Parker, Psychologist*

"Don't try to blend in…blend out."

~*Lesego, student from Oprah's Leadership Academy*

"Most people give up what they want most, for what
they want in the moment."

~*Matt Fakhouri, Student, Henry Ford Community College*

"If you have Faith, God works in obvious ways."

~*Gary Martin, "Up & Coming" Entrepreneur*

"There's a door that has opened, and now there's one
that needs to close."

~*Kinzel Forrest, Sales Manager*

"Let somebody know you been here."

~*William Beckham Sr.,
Former UAW Administrative Assistant*

"If you go through life and you never learned anything, it was all just a waste."

~*Barry Martin, Plant Operations Assistant*

"Stop looking at the circumstances and look at the Word."

~*Alicia Phillips, Wife, Mother and Grandmother*

"It's not about how long we live, but what we do with our life, while we're here."

~*Charnette, Cancer patient from the Oprah Winfrey Show*

"It's alright to have a pity party, but know when to end the party."

~*Erma Wilson, Mother and Grandmother*

"It is in our mistakes that we have the most opportunity for growing and healing."

~*Carla Jankowski, College Professor*

"Tell the truth, because it's the right thing to do."

~*Mildred Gaddis, Journalist*

"If it can be done, you can do it; it's a matter of choice."

~*Marian Robinson,*
President Barack Obama's Mother-in-Law

Embrace YOUR gifts."
~*T.M.*

III.
A Celebrity's "Take"

Despite our distinctly varied paths, lifestyles and occupations, we all have a commonality—we are ALL members of the human race, and it is because of that, that we are able to offer uniquely different, yet attested philosophical views/experiences on mankind.

So as you read about the *Celebrity's "Take"*, check out the similarities between their take and yours...trust me...you'll be surprised...or maybe not?...just read on.

"A wise man changes, a fool never changes."

~*Judge Mablean*

"Your attitude determines your altitude."

~*Les Brown, Motivational Speaker*

"You are not what you have been, but the possibility of what you can be."

~*Oprah Winfrey, Talk Show Host*

"If you always do what you always did, you will always get what you always got."

~*"Moms" Mabley, Comedian*

"Your life is bigger than you know."

~*Oprah Winfrey, Talk Show Host*

"The difference between winners and losers, winners do things, losers don't want to do."

~*Dr. Phil McGraw, Talk Show Host*

"God uses good people to do great things."

~*Oprah Winfrey, Talk Show Host*

"The best predictor of future behavior, is past behavior…so you gotta create a new history."

~*Dr. Phil McGraw, Talk Show Host*

"Whenever you have to consult with other people for an answer, you're headed in the wrong direction."

~*Oprah Winfrey, Talk Show Host*

"God is everything, without God, you ain't got nothing."

~*Steve Harvey, Comedian*

"Man gives you the award and God gives you the reward."

~*Denzel Washington, Actor*

"Joy and Depression can not reside in the same place."

~*Steve Harvey, Comedian*

"I am the lucky person, because I love my life and I know I love my life."

~Ed Bradley, Journalist

"Being poor is not who you are, it's just a circumstance."

~Oprah Winfrey, Talk Show Host

"You have to allow life to play itself out."

~Helen Mirren, Actress

"May all your storms get weathered and all your good, get better."

~Liz Wright, Jazz Singer

"The future belongs to those who prepare for it today."

~Malcolm X, Civil Rights Activist

"The people that are winners in this life are the people that just go for it."

~Howie Mandel, Actor/Comedian

"If you have that drive, keep going."

~Jaslene, " America's Next Top Model"(winner, 2007)

"If you let your fears keep you from flying, you will never reach your height."

~India Arie, Singer & Songwriter

"Nothing in the world is more dangerous than sincere ignorance and conscientious stupidity."

~Dr. Martin Luther King, Jr., Civil Rights Activist

"It is how you handle the failing that determines your success in life."

~Steve Harvey, Comedian

"Decide that you want it more than you are afraid of it."

~Bill Cosby, Actor & Comedian

"If you fall, fall on your back. If you can look up, you can get up."

~Les Brown, Motivational Speaker

"Don't worry, be happy."

~*Bobby McFerrin, Singer*

"You survived 100,000 other sperm to get here. What do you mean you don't know what to do?"

~*Les Brown, Motivational Speaker*

"Above all, don't fear difficult moments…the best comes from them."

~*Rita Levi Montalcini, Nobel Prize Winning Scientist*

"When it's all said and done,
we have more similarities than differences."
~T.M.

IV.
A Writer's Perspective

The written word—I absolutely love it—I can't get enough of it, as it opens the door to a world of wonderful possibilities, for those brave enough to enter. So I challenge you to broaden your horizons, by continuing on this literary journey, by "gifting" yourself with continued reading...*go ahead...just walk through the door...your future is on the other side...you won't be disappointed...provided, you've made the choice to avoid the...***"Yeah But Syndrome"***...the choice is yours.*

"Don't give in to your fears…If you do, you won't be
able to talk to your heart. There is only one thing
that makes a dream impossible to achieve: the fear
of failure."

~Paulo Coelho, Author

"If you just intellectually believe something, but you
have no corresponding feeling underneath that, you
don't necessarily have enough power to manifest
what you want in your life. You have to feel it."

~Dr. Michael Bernard Beckwith, founder of the Agape In-
ternational Spiritual Center & Author

"I have learned that if one advances confidently in the
direction of his dreams, and endeavors to live the
life he has imagined, he will meet with a success
unexpected in common hours."

~Henry David Thoreau, Writer

"We need a CHANGE…We have to have a
CHANGE."

~Michael Baisden, Radio Talk Show Host & Author

"Never forget that this is your one precious life. *Your* life. And you have the power to create your future. If you don't like the path you're taking, why in the world would you continue down that road?"

~Robin Roberts, Co-Anchor of Good Morning America & Author

"God and the Universe will conspire to give you what you go after as long as you are clear on what you want and work hard for it."

~Hill Harper, Actor and Author

"To be given a gift is a reward, to utilize it is a blessing. So no matter how painful life is at any moment, no matter what difficulty you are going through, if you can look at it through your divine spirit, you can appreciate it and grow from it."

~Natasha Munson, Motivational Speaker and Author

"Believe that if you wish for something, it can happen. Believe that you *can* be the "somebody" you wished you could be."

~Squire Rushnell, Author

"When I stand before God at the end of my life, I would hope that I would not have a single bit of talent left, and could say, I used everything You gave me."

~Erma Bombeck, Author

"You are most powerful, most effective, when you are completely yourself. But don't try to be yourself. That's another role. It's called "natural, spontaneous me." As soon as you are trying to be this or that, you are playing a role. "Just be yourself..."

~Eckhart Tolle, Spiritual Teacher and Author

"You don't have to be a Writer, to tell your story—
by simply living your life to it's fullest,
you're telling your story—each and every day."
~T.M.

V.
The "Inside-Out" Job

Over the years, I've learned that the development of personal joy and happiness, is not achieved on the outside of oneself; instead, it must begin on the "inside", where the foundation for personal growth is first cultivated. Sadly, many people lack this understanding, as they often look "outside" of themselves for their personal joy and happiness. I've also learned and truly believe that one of the reasons we have other people in our lives, is to compliment each other. They are not to *complete* us, as so many people also believe. Just think about it, to have another person complete YOU, gives them a wealth of responsibility, control and power. Quite frankly that's just too much power to give away. In other words, we must tell our own stories and develop our own endings…it's your life, so you must be the *"completer"* of your own stories.

So go ahead…read on, and arm yourself with the courage to see how it's done.

"We all need to be very clear that the love in our lives begins with us."

~Louise L. Hay, Author

"If you are not for you
Who will be?
If you are only for you
What's the purpose?
If not now, when?"

~Hillel, Poet

"If you do not value your own Being you cannot cherish others. Improving your relationship to yourself is where the action is. The treasure you seek lies within."

~Dorothy Corkville-Briggs, Author

"We help another person access their highest, by accessing our own. Growth comes from focus on our own lessons, not on someone else's."

~Marianne Williamson, Author

"You must be the change you wish to see in the world."

~*Mahatma Gandhi*

"I am a true believer in the power of self. And without self-love there's no self-confidence. Without self-confidence there's no respect."

~*Lauren London, Actress*

"It's easy to believe that if someone else loves you, it means that you're somehow more lovable. But that's just not true. Good feelings about yourself can only come from the inside."

~*Tatyana Ali, Actress*

"...when you stand up, when you make your voice heard, then people listen to you, people stand with you, people want to work with you and you are that much closer to taking your seat at the table."

~*Michelle Obama, First Lady of the United States of America*

"Never depend on anyone else for your happiness."

~*Susan L. Taylor, Author*

"...but what freed me to be me was the understanding of how to tuck a part of me away from me. And not let anyone define who I am."

~Nikki Giovanni, Poet & Author

"Begin to weave and God will give you the thread."

~German Proverb

"Shoot for the moon, and the worst that can happen, you'll land among the stars."

~Tony Orlando, Singer

"All I have seen teaches me to trust the creator for all I have not seen."

~Ralph Waldo Emerson, Author

"Other people do not have to change for us to experience peace of mind."

~Gerald G. Jampolsky, Medical Doctor & Author

"If you are alive, there is hope for a better day and
  something good to happen."

~*Ishmael Beah, Author*

"Living your truth means behaving as the most truthful
  representation of who you are."

~*Hill Harper, Actor & Author*

"…being defeated is a temporary condition. Giving up is
  what makes it permanent."

~*Barack Obama, President of the United States of America*

"Devote yourself to loving others, devote yourself to
  your community around you, and devote yourself to
  creating something that gives you purpose and
  meaning."

~*Mitch Albom, Author*

"Your work is to discover your work and then with all
  your heart, give yourself to it."

~*Buddha*

"When you have faith in yourself, you—the you who knows your own greatness—stands up to the doubts."

~Lisa Nichols, Motivational Speaker & Author

"The future belongs to those who believe in the beauty of their dreams."

~Eleanor Roosevelt, Former First Lady of the United States of America

"The moment you make a real decision, the change happens instantly."

~Kurek Ashley, Actor & Author

"Be what you want to see!"

~Carolyn Cheeks Kilpatrick, Congresswoman

"You can not belong to anyone else, until you belong to yourself".

~Pearl Bailey, Singer, Dancer & Actress

"All conditions and all circumstances in our lives are the result of a certain level of thinking. When you want to change the conditions and the circumstances, we have to change the level of thinking that is responsible for it."

~Albert Einstein

"The work starts with YOU."
~T.M.

VI.
The "Joint" Effort

For as long as I can remember, I have been interested in people and how they interact in relationships, specifically intimate relationships. What intrigues me the most is how people talk about wanting a relationship and being an ideal mate, but they are often single and alone. Curiously, if people are interested in having a relationship and believe they are ideal mates, why aren't they in a relationship? With that question, I felt driven to write about those things necessary to successfully live in and achieve the *"Joint" effort*. This is simply, the work required to obtain and maintain, happy and healthy intimate relationships.

So go ahead…read on, the work doesn't stop here, remain courageous, as you learn to embrace the power of two.

"…for relationships to really work, we need to focus on what we appreciate about the other person, not what we're complaining about."

~*Marci Shimoff, Author*

"There is no formula to relationships. They have to be negotiated in loving ways, with room for both parties, what they want and what they need, what they can do and what their life is like."

~*Morrie Schwartz, Professor*

"We want the bountiful rain but not the thunder, the treasures of the ocean but not it's awful roar."

~*Frederick Douglass, Antislavery Activist & Orator*

"Relationships bring what we're open to receiving."

~*Susan L. Taylor, Author*

"You have to help each other know who you are. You have to sanction each other's gifts and encourage each other."

~*Ruby Dee, Actress*

"Black children will continue to catch hell as long as we don't partner better or love each other better. And until building healthy relationships becomes a priority, we won't be able to handle the challenges undermining our progress."

~*Cornel West, Scholar & Author*

"A healthy relationship stretches us into growing the areas that are emotionally, spiritually, and physically underdeveloped."

~*Dr. Robin L. Smith, Psychotherapist & Author*

"A relationship is not meant to be joining at the hip of two emotional invalids. The purpose of a relationship is not for two incomplete people to become one, but rather for two complete people to join together for the greater glory of God."

~*Marianne Williamson, Author*

"A relationship is placing one's heart and soul in the hands of another while taking charge of another in one's soul and heart."

~*Kahlil Gibran, Author*

"Imagine what a harmonious world it could be if every single person, both young and old, shared a little of what he is good at doing."

~Quincy Jones, Musician

"...we need relationships and in particular we need the kind of committed long-term relationships that allow us to heal and grow."

~Dr. Harville Hendrix, Developer of Imago Therapy

"Believe in the power of TWO."
~T.M.

VII.
God's Words

Because I accept God as the head of my life, I would be remiss, if I did not include and dedicate a section of this book to my *Heavenly Father*. So in this last chapter, and most important section of the book, I've included scriptures from the *Bible* that I deem to be thought-provoking, inspirational and invigorating. So continue on, as you conclude this "spiritual journey", on how to avoid the *"Yeah But Syndrome."* Always remember to—*Keep the FAITH* and trust the process, and know that your healing is on the way.

All Biblical verses in the current chapter and throughout this book were taken from the Holy Bible (King James Version, 1979)

"Keep thy heart with all diligence; for out of it are the issues of life."

~Proverbs 4:23-24

"Behold, I will do a new thing; now it shall spring forth; shall ye not know it? I will even make a way in the wilderness, *and* rivers in the desert."

~Isaiah 43:19

"Put on the whole armour of God that ye may be able to stand against the wiles of the devil."

~Ephesians 6:11

"Be careful for nothing; but in every thing by prayer and supplication with thanksgiving let your requests be made known unto God."

~Philippians 4:6

"Therefore if any man *be* in Christ, *he is* a new creature: old things are passed away; behold, all things are become new."

~2 Corinthians 6:17

"Rejoicing in hope; patient in tribulation; continuing instant in prayer."

~Romans 12:12

"…be not faithless, but believing."

~John 20:27

"And seek not ye what ye shall eat, or what ye shall drink, neither be ye of doubtful mind."

~Luke 12:29

"…Be strong and of a good courage, be not afraid, neither be thou dismayed; for the Lord thy God is with thee whithersoever thou goest."

~Joshua 1:9

"…Be not afraid, only believe."

~Mark 5:36

"…I *am* with you, saith the Lord."

~Haggai 1:13

"…Fear not."

~*Lamentations 3:57*

"Where *there is* no vision, the people perish; but he that
keepeth the law, happy is he."

~*Proverbs 29:18*

"My flesh and my heart faileth; *but* God *is* the strength
of my heart, and my portion forever."

~*Psalms 73:26*

"Be of good courage…"

~*2 Samuel 10:12*

"I will fear no evil: for thou art with me…"

~*Psalm 23:4*

"And now, my daughter, fear not; I will do to thee all
that thou requirest…"

~*Ruth 3:11*

"For God hath not given us the spirit of fear; but of power, and of love, and of a sound mind."

~Timothy 1:7

"...Lord God of thy fathers hath said unto thee: fear not, neither be discouraged."

~Deuteronomy 1:21

"...because greater is he that is in you, than he that is in the world."

~I John 4:4

"For the vision *is* yet for an appointed time, but at the end it shall speak, and not lie: though it tarry, wait for it; because it will surely come, it will not tarry."

~Habakkuk 2:3

"The Lord is not slack concerning his promises, as some men count slackness..."

~2 Peter 3:9

"Ask, and it shall be given you..."

~Matthew 7:7

"But let every man prove his own work, and then shall he have rejoicing in himself alone, and not in another."

~Galatians 6:4

"But wilt thou know, O vain man, that faith without works is dead ?"

~James 2:20

"But without faith *it is* impossible to please *him*: for he that cometh to God must believe that he is, and *that* he is a rewarder of them that diligently seek him."

~Hebrews 11:6

"But the Lord is faithful, who shall stablish you, and keep you from evil."

~II Thessalonians 3:3

"HE said it--so that makes it so."
~T.M.

Afterword

It is my hope and prayer that You—the person having read this book, will be able to incorporate some or at least one of the many quotes or scriptures, into your daily life, as a prescription, on how to effectively avoid and/or rid yourself of the *"Yeah But Syndrome."* All it takes—is the willingness, desire and courage to---*STOP saying, "YEAH, BUT" and START DOING!"*

"Show and live the life YOU desire to see."
~T.M.

Closing Quote

"When you're no longer afraid of hurt or failure and
   have stopped breathing life into your insecurities,
   then greatness can appear."

~Lisa Nichols, Author & Motivational Speaker

Acknowledgments

I must first thank my *Heavenly Father*, for giving me the vision and courage to write this book.

I also express much Love and Thanks to *my Mom*, for *always, always, always* "having my back".

I give Thanks to *my brother, Barry*, for his quiet, yet glowing show of love and support.

BIG Thanks! to my *sister, Leslie*, for always being my number one Cheerleader.

I say—THANK YOU, THANK YOU, THANK YOU, to my *dear, dear friends—Alicia, Pam and Kinzel* for more than **two decades** of friendship…what we have is everlasting!

Charles Beckham, THANK YOU! for your many *"Beckhamisms"*, as they've been astoundingly humorous, educational and enlightening, but above all else—amazing teaching tools.

Melva and Jesse, I Thank You! for your loving, mentoring spirit…you have been a true Blessing to me.

Dr. Pauline Furman, Thank You! for your professional and personal friendship…it has been priceless.

I'd also like to Thank, *my many clients and students*, for your inquisitive minds and willingness to make a *positive change* in your lives, by doing different, because you wanted different.

Dr. Fischetti, Thank You! for the informative, concise and educational supervision—you've "gifted" me with a wealth of knowledge.

THANKS! to my *"Positive Change"* group members, for having the fortitude and curiosity, to trust me and the process…you epitomize *"Positive Change"*.

Tremendous Thanks, to my Editor, *Dr. Dawn Bielawski* for your careful and meticulous review of this document, as you and your expertise, have been an absolute blessing.

Rev. Foster, your support comes from a truly rich and genuine place, and I say—THANK YOU! for being YOU.

Sincere Thanks! *Rev. Reid,* for your faithful leadership & guidance…you are a *true* man of God.

www.ingramcontent.com/pod-product-compliance
Lightning Source LLC
Chambersburg PA
CBHW071022040426
42443CB00007B/902